Introducing...

THE HA HA HANDBOOK

101 Days of FUN!

Only turn this page if you like jokes...

For my 3rd
grade students
at Imagine
who love a
good joke!

DAY 1
day one

How does a penguin build a house?

Igloos it together!

WOULD YOU RATHER... HAVE SPAGHETTI HAIR OR MARSHMALLOW TOES?

FUN FACT: Butterflies taste things with their FEET!

DAY 2
day two

Why are frogs always happy?

They eat what bugs them!

FUN FACT:
A bolt of lightning is 5 times hotter than the sun!

WOULD YOU RATHER... SNEEZE EVERY TIME YOU SAY HELLO OR HICCUP EVERY TIME YOU SAY GOODBYE?

DAY 3
day three

WOULD YOU RATHER... HAVE AN ELEPHANT-SIZED HAMSTER OR A HAMSTER-SIZED ELEPHANT?

FUN FACT: A hippo's lips are almost 2 feet long!

What do you call a blind dinosaur?

do-you-think-he-saur-us

DAY 4
day four

What do you call a cow that eats your grass?

A lawn moo-er.

WOULD YOU RATHER... HAVE EYES THAT HONK WHEN YOU BLINK OR SHOES THAT QUACK WHEN YOU WALK?

FUN FACT: It's impossible to hum while holding your nose!

DAY 5
day five

Why are pigs bad drivers ?

They hog the road!

FUN FACT: Bananas are berries but strawberries are not!

WOULD YOU RATHER... SING INSTEAD OF SPEAKING OR DANCE INSTEAD OF WALKING?

DAY 6
day six

WOULD YOU RATHER... BE FOLLOWED BY A FLOCK OF CHICKENS OR A HERD OF GOATS?

FUN FACT: Human ears and noses never stop growing.

How do you throw a party in space?

You planet early.

DAY 7
day seven

What did one ocean say to the other ocean?

Nothing, it waved.

WOULD YOU RATHER... HAVE SUPER STRENGTH OR SUPER SPEED?

FUN FACT: A sneeze can travel at a speed of 100mph!

DAY 8
day eight

What happens when a jellyfish eats too much?

It gets a jelly-ache!

FUN FACT: Abraham Lincoln was a champion wrestler!

WOULD YOU RATHER... HAVE BUTTERFLY WINGS OR A HORSE TAIL?

DAY 9
day nine

WOULD YOU RATHER... HAVE A T-REX OR AN ALLIGATOR AS A HOUSE PET?

FUN FACT:
A Stegosaurus had a brain the size of a walnut!

What is a boxer's favorite drink?

Fruit Punch

DAY 10
day ten

What do you call a sheep that does karate?

Lambchop

WOULD YOU RATHER... WEAR A CLOWN WIG OR A CLOWN NOSE TO SCHOOL?

FUN FACT: Giraffes pick their nose with their tongues!

DAY 11
day eleven

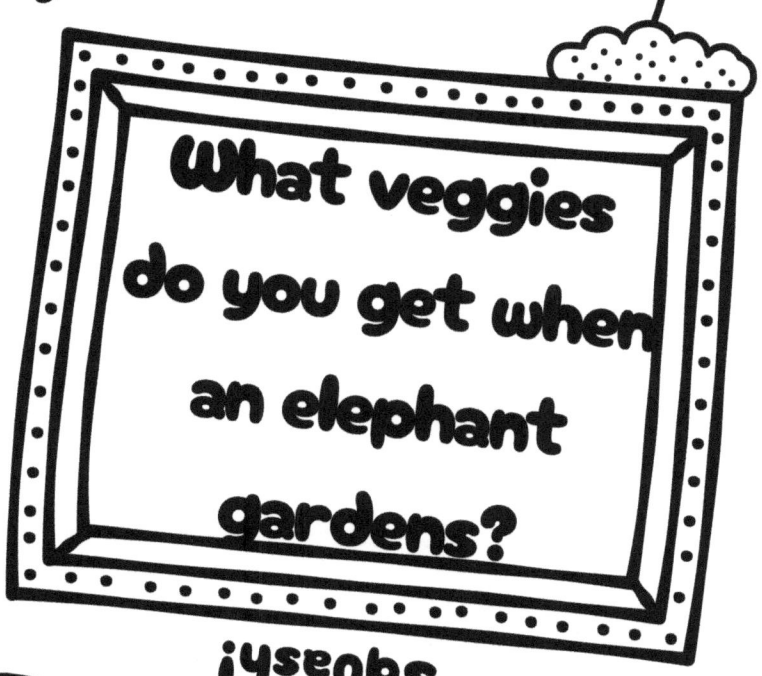

What veggies do you get when an elephant gardens?

i4senbs

FUN FACT: Sharks don't have any bones, only cartilage!

WOULD YOU RATHER... BREATHE UNDERWATER OR FLY LIKE A BIRD?

DAY 12
day twelve

FUN FACT:
Bats have thumbs!

WOULD YOU RATHER... HAVE CRAB CLAW HANDS OR WEBBED FEET LIKE A DUCK?

What has a tail and head but no body?

A coin.

DAY 13
day thirteen

What letter in the alphabet has the most water?

WOULD YOU RATHER... BURP WHEN YOU WALK OR FART WHEN YOU RUN?

FUN FACT: Flamingos turn their head upside down to eat!

DAY 14
day fourteen

Why did the bicycle fall over?

¡It was two tired!

FUN FACT: Ants can lift 20 times their own body weight!

WOULD YOU RATHER... HAVE A NOSE LIKE A PIG OR A TAIL LIKE A MONKEY?

DAY 15
day fifteen

FUN FACT: The closest living relative to a t-rex is a chicken!

WOULD YOU RATHER... WEAR HAMBURGER SHOES OR A HOTDOG HAT?

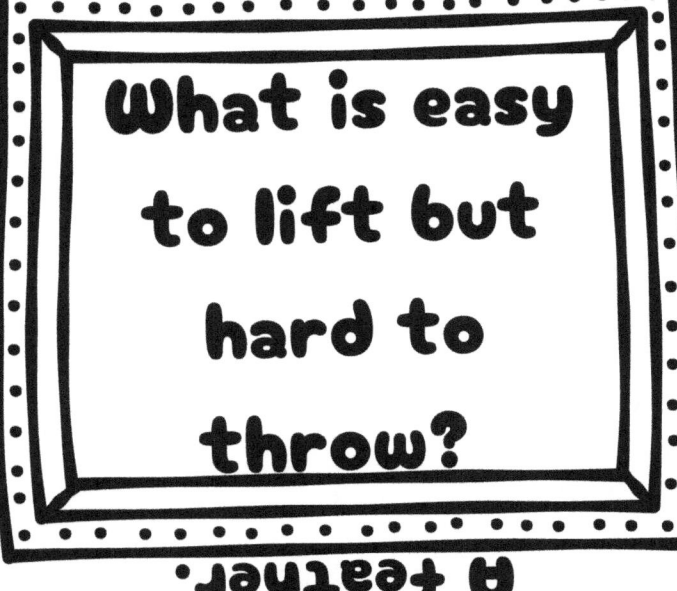

What is easy to lift but hard to throw?

A feather.

DAY 16
day sixteeen

Where will you find Friday before Thursday?

A dictionary.

WOULD YOU RATHER...
EAT A RAW POTATO OR A RAW ONION?

FUN FACT:
koala Bears aren't bears, they are marsupials!

DAY 17
day seventeen

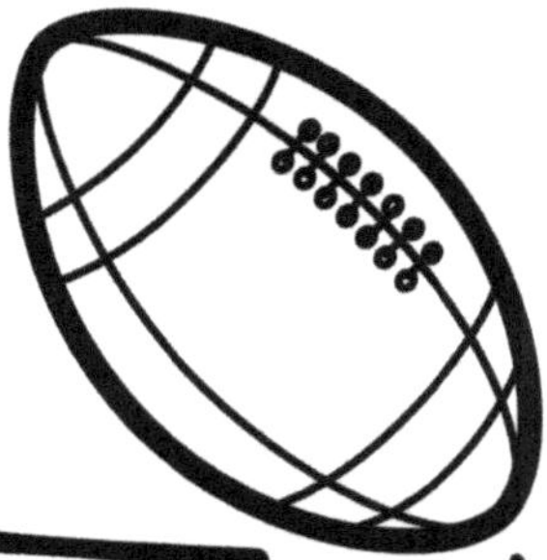

Why is the football field the coolest place to be?

Because it's full of fans!

FUN FACT:
Your eyes move around when you are dreaming!

WOULD YOU RATHER... FIND HIDDEN TREASURE OR GET THREE WISHES?

DAY 18
day eighteen

WOULD YOU RATHER... LIVE WITHOUT A PHONE OR A COMPUTER?

FUN FACT: Cats have three eyelids!

Why do bees have sticky hair?

They use a honeycomb!

DAY 19
day nineteen

What kind of car does a sheep drive?

A Lamborghini!

WOULD YOU RATHER... BE ABLE TO ONLY SHOUT OR ONLY WHISPER?

FUN FACT: Some giraffes only sleep 30 minutes a day!

DAY 20
day twenty

Why did the coach go to the bank?

To get his quarter back!

FUN FACT: The average nose makes about a cupful of mucus daily!

WOULD YOU RATHER... HAVE TWO LONG GREEN FRONT TEETH OR NO TEETH AT ALL?

DAY 21
day twenty-one

WOULD YOU RATHER... HAVE STINKY BREATH OR STINKY ARMPITS?

FUN FACT: The longest fingernails in the world were 42 feet!

Why are spiders so smart?

They search the web for answers!

DAY 22
day twenty-two

What do you call a fibbing cat?

A lion.

WOULD YOU RATHER...
BE A CLUMSY NINJA OR A WIZARD THAT CAN'T REMEMBER ANYTHING?

FUN FACT:
Bananas glow blue under a black light!

DAY 23
day twenty-three

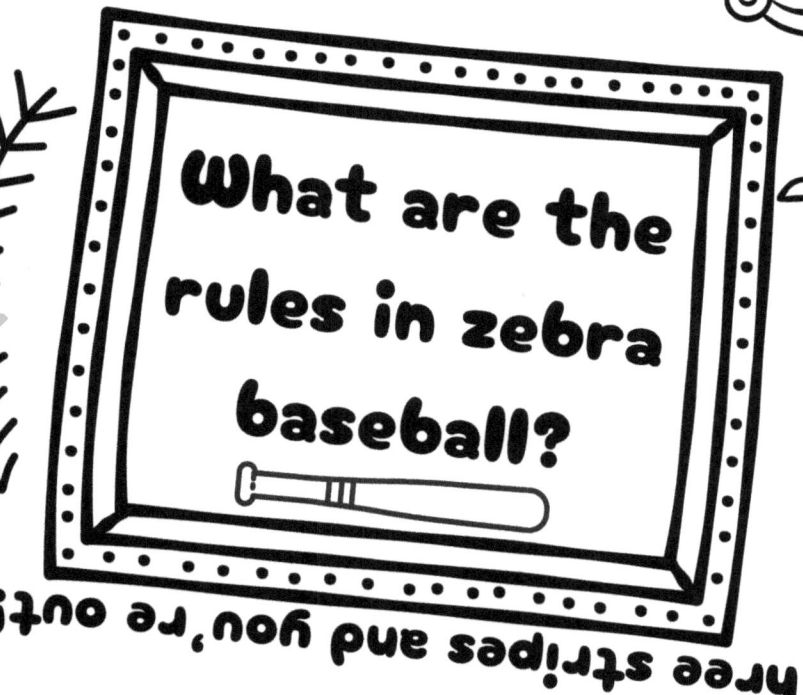

What are the rules in zebra baseball?

Three stripes and you're out!

FUN FACT: President Roosevelt had a pet hyena!

WOULD YOU RATHER... HAVE A ROBOT THAT DOES HOMEWORK OR A ROBOT THAT CLEANS YOUR ROOM?

DAY 24
day twenty-four

FUN FACT:
A blue whale's tongue can weigh as much as an elephant!

WOULD YOU RATHER...
GO A MONTH WITHOUT INTERNET OR A MONTH WITHOUT BATHING?

What do you call a lazy kangaroo?

A pouch potato.

DAY 25
day twenty-five

What do you call it when a snowman throws a fit?

A meltdown.

WOULD YOU RATHER...
BE COVERED IN FUR OR COVERED IN FEATHERS?

FUN FACT:
The only food that can never go bad is honey!

DAY 26
day twenty-six

What do you call a dinosaur that crashed his car?

T-wrecks.

FUN FACT: The first animal to ever be cloned is a sheep!

WOULD YOU RATHER... BE PRESIDENT OF THE UNITED STATES OR KING/QUEEN OF THE WORLD?

DAY 27
day twenty-seven

WOULD YOU RATHER... NEVER EAT CANDY OR NEVER EAT PIZZA EVER AGAIN?

FUN FACT: The national animal of Scotland is a unicorn!

What did the left eye say to the right eye?

Something smells!

DAY 28
day twenty-eight

Where do trees go to learn?

Elemen-tree school.

WOULD YOU RATHER... SLEEP ON THE FLOOR FOREVER OR EAT ONLY CRACKERS FOREVER?

FUN FACT: The first iPod was released in 2001.

DAY 29
day twenty-nine

What do you call a bear without teeth?

Gummy bear.

FUN FACT: The earth spins about 1000mph.

WOULD YOU RATHER... BE A MILLIONAIRE WHO ALWAYS STAYS HOME OR A TRAVELER WHO IS POOR?

DAY 30
day thirty

FUN FACT:
Turtles can breathe through their butts!

WOULD YOU RATHER... LIVE BY A NOISY TRAIN STATION OR A STINKY LANDFILL?

What do squirrels watch on t.v.?

Nut-flix

DAY 31
day thirty-one

Who is the superhero in computer class?

The screensaver.

WOULD YOU RATHER... HAVE AN EXTRA EYE OR AN EXTRA EAR?

FUN FACT: Neptune has 14 moons!

DAY 32
day thirty-two

Why do hummingbirds hum?

They don't know the words!

FUN FACT: Crickets have ears on their legs!

WOULD YOU RATHER... BE ABLE TO TALK TO PLANTS OR TALK TO ANIMALS?

DAY 33
day thirty-three

FUN FACT:
A macaroni penguin has yellow feathers on top of its head!

WOULD YOU RATHER...
EAT DOG FOOD THAT TASTE LIKE CAKE OR CAKE THAT TASTE LIKE DOG FOOD?

How do you keep a bull from charging?

Take away his credit card!

DAY 34
day thirty-four

What do you call an alligator who solves crimes?

An investigator!

WOULD YOU RATHER... HAVE HICCUPS FOR A WEEK OR SNEEZE FOR A WEEK?

FUN FACT: The first telephone call was in 1876!

DAY 35
day thirty-five

What kind of room does not have any doors?

A mushroom.

FUN FACT: The first text message was in 1992!

WOULD YOU RATHER... RIDE ON A FLYING CARPET OR A FLYING UNICORN?

DAY 36
day thirty-six

FUN FACT: Bulldog ants are the most dangerous ant on the planet.

WOULD YOU RATHER... HAVE A SUPERPOWER THAT MAKES YOU INVISIBLE OR MAKES YOU FLY?

Where do fruit go on vacation?

Pear-is.

DAY 37
day thirty-seven

How do you know if a flower is friendly?

It has a lot of buds!

WOULD YOU RATHER... SOUND LIKE A COW WHEN YOU LAUGH OR SOUND LIKE A CHICKEN?

FUN FACT: Male horseflies can fly up to 90 mph!

DAY 38
day thirty-eight

Why can't you trust a taco?

They always spill the beans!

FUN FACT: Florida is the flattest state in America!

WOULD YOU RATHER... BE AN ASTRONAUT OR A PALENTOLOGIST?

DAY 39
day thirty-nine

FUN FACT: Manatees eat plants but can weigh about 3,000 pounds!

WOULD YOU RATHER... HAVE NO HOMEWORK OR NO TESTS?

What kind of vegetable is angry?

A steamed carrot

DAY 40
day forty

How do you get an astronaut's baby to sleep?

You rocket.

WOULD YOU RATHER...
BE TRANSPORTED TO THE FUTURE OR TO THE PAST?

FUN FACT:
Kangaroos can be as tall or taller than an adult!

DAY 41
day forty-one

What is a rabbit's favorite kind of music?

Hip Hop.

FUN FACT:
A trip to Pluto in an airplane would take 800 years!

WOULD YOU RATHER...
HAVE 10 SISTERS OR 10 BROTHERS?

DAY 42
day forty-two

WOULD YOU RATHER... HAVE A GIANT PET SPIDER OR A GIANT PET SNAKE?

FUN FACT: Every minute you shed over 30,000 dead skin cells!

What is a snake's favorite subject?

Hisssss-tory.

DAY 43
day forty-three

Why isn't there a clock in the library?

It locks too much!

WOULD YOU RATHER... BE YOUR TEACHER FOR THE DAY OR YOUR PARENT FOR THE DAY?

FUN FACT: Abraham Lincoln was the tallest president!

???

DAY 44
day forty-four

What contest did he skunk win at school?

The smelling bee!

FUN FACT: Saturn's rings are made of chunks of ice, rocks, & dust!

WOULD YOU RATHER... EAT FRENCH FRIES WITH WHIP CREAM OR ICE CREAM WITH KETCHUP?

DAY 45
day forty-five

WOULD YOU RATHER... LIVE ON THE MOON OR LIVE UNDERWATER?

FUN FACT: The oldest president to be elected is Joe Biden.

What did the baker say when she won an award?

It was a piece of cake!

DAY 46
day forty-six

Why did the baseball player go to jail?

He stole 2nd base!

WOULD YOU RATHER... WASH DISHES FOR A MONTH OR CLEAN BATHROOMS FOR A WEEK?

FUN FACT: The oldest sport in the world is wrestling!

DAY 47
day forty-seven

How does the
Easter Bunny
stay in shape?

Lots of eggs-ercise!

FUN FACT:
The longest
dog tongue
was about 5.5
inches.

WOULD YOU
RATHER...
BRUSH YOUR
TEETH WITH
SOUP OR BRUSH
YOUR TEETH
WITH COFFEE?

DAY 48
day forty-eight

MILK

FUN FACT:
The world's longest french fry was 34 inches!

WOULD YOU RATHER... EAT A ROTTEN EGG OR DRINK A GLASS OF SPOILED MILK?

Where do hamburgers go to dance?

The meatball.

DAY 49
day forty-nine

Which vegetable is the most kind?

The sweet potato!

WOULD YOU RATHER... ALWAYS WALK ON YOUR HANDS AND FEET OR ALWAYS WALK BACKWARDS?

FUN FACT: There are 2000 thunderstorms on Earth every minute!

DAY 50
day fifty

What did the
diamond say
to her friend?

"You're a gem!"

FUN FACT:
Human teeth
are as strong
as shark
teeth!

WOULD YOU
RATHER...
USE ONLY YOUR
HANDS TO EAT
EVERYTHING OR
USE CHOPSTICKS
TO EAT
EVERYTHING?

DAY 51
day fifty-one

FUN FACT: Our body has 206 bones. The smallest is in the ear.

WOULD YOU RATHER... HAVE PURPLE AND PINK EYES OR PURPLE AND PINK HAIR?

How do trees go on the internet?

They log in.

DAY 52
day fifty-two

What do you call a can opener that doesn't open?

A can't opener.

WOULD YOU RATHER... RIDE AROUND ON A DONKEY OR DRIVE A CLOWN CAR?

FUN FACT: Earthworms have five hearts!

DAY 53
day fifty-three

What do lawyers wear to work?

Lawsuits.

FUN FACT: The average adult brain weighs 3 pounds!

WOULD YOU RATHER... BE A FAMOUS SINGER OR FAMOUS ATHLETE?

DAY 54
day fifty-four

FUN FACT:
Sheep have rectangular pupils!

WOULD YOU RATHER... HAVE ONE HUGE MUSCLE ON YOUR ARM OR A LONG CURL OF HAIR ON YOUR KNEE?

What did the baseball glove say to the baseball?

"Catch you later!"

DAY 55
day fifty-five

What is the best time to go to the dentist?

Tooth-hurty.

WOULD YOU RATHER... LIVE IN A CARTOON OR LIVE IN A VIDEO GAME?

FUN FACT: Humans are made up of more than 60% water.

DAY 56
day fifty-six

Why should you tell jokes to a duck?

They always quack up!

FUN FACT:
1 million Earths could fit inside the sun!

WOULD YOU RATHER... LIVE ON A PRIVATE ISLAND OR LIVE ON A STRANDED BOAT?

DAY 57
day fifty-seven

FUN FACT:
Red is the first color a baby can see!

WOULD YOU RATHER... OWN A CHOCOLATE FACTORY OR A LEGO FACTORY?

What do kids play when they have nothing to do?

Bored games.

DAY 58
day fifty-eight

What does a librarian use to go fishing?

A bookworm.

WOULD YOU RATHER... SWITCH FOOD WITH YOUR DOG FOR A DAY OR EAT BROCCOLI FOR A WEEK?

FUN FACT: Potatoes were the first vegetable to grow in space!

DAY 59
day fifty-nine

What do you call a rude cow?

Beef Jerky.

HA HA HA HA!

FUN FACT: President Roosevelt named The White House!

WOULD YOU RATHER... HAVE A PERFECT MEMORY OR TELL THE FUNNIEST JOKES?

DAY 60
day sixty

WOULD YOU RATHER... GIVE AWAY HALF OF YOUR TOYS OR GIVE UP CANDY FOR A YEAR?

FUN FACT: An octopus has 9 brains and 3 hearts!

Why can't Cinderella play baseball?

She runs away from the ball!

DAY 61
day sixty-one

How do birds learn how to fly?

They wing it!

WOULD YOU RATHER... HAVE $5 NOW OR $10 NEXT WEEK?

FUN FACT: When you are scared, your pupils get larger!

DAY 62
day sixty-two

How did the
barber win
the race?

He knew a shortcut!

FUN FACT:
Clouds look
white because
they reflect
sunlight!

WOULD YOU
RATHER...
WALK LIKE A
PENGUIN OR
SLITHER LIKE A
SNAKE?

DAY 63
day sixty-three

FUN FACT: Panda bears mostly eat bamboo!

WOULD YOU RATHER... HAVE A RAINBOW COLORED TONGUE OR POLKA-DOTTED EARS?

Where do armies belong?

In your sleevies!

DAY 64
day sixty-four

What do you call a group of giraffes on a busy street?

A giraff-ic jam!

WOULD YOU RATHER... SOUND LIKE MICKEY MOUSE OR SOUND LIKE DONALD DUCK?

FUN FACT: Foxes use their tail to communicate to other foxes!

DAY 65
day sixty-five

What is the most popular fish in the ocean?

The starfish.

FUN FACT: Identical twins do not have the same fingerprints!

WOULD YOU RATHER... HAVE A LONG BEARD OR EXTRA TOES ON YOUR FEET?

DAY 66
day sixty-six

>>>>>>

FUN FACT:
The world's oldest dog was 29.5 years old!

WOULD YOU RATHER...
BE ABLE TO WALK THROUGH WALLS ON WALK ON THE CEILING?

Why do sharks swim in salt water?

Pepper water makes them sneeze!

DAY 67
day sixty-seven

What did the 0 say to the 8?

Nice belt!

WOULD YOU RATHER... NEVER EAT ICE CREAM OR NEVER EAT PIZZA?

FUN FACT: The world's oldest cat was 38 years old!

DAY 68
day sixty-eight

How do you
make a
sausage roll?

Push it down a hill!

FUN FACT:
Snails have
thousands of
microscopic
teeth!

WOULD YOU
RATHER...
HAVE ONE TINY
EYE OR ONE
TINY HAND?

DAY 69
day sixty-nine

WOULD YOU RATHER... RIDE A SKATEBOARD EVERYWHERE YOU GO OR RIDE A HORSE?

FUN FACT: Hippos can't swim!

Why was the math book sad?

It had too many problems!

DAY 70
day seventy

Why did the golfer bring an extra pair of socks?

In case he gets a hole in one!

WOULD YOU RATHER... WEAR A CROWN MADE OF PIZZA SLICES OR A JACKET MADE OF PANCAKES?

FUN FACT: The smallest bird is the Bee Hummingbird!

DAY 71
day seventy-one

What is a ghost's favorite ride?

A roller ghost-er!

FUN FACT: The smallest organ is in your brain, the pineal gland!

WOULD YOU RATHER... BE STICKY LIKE SYRUP FOR A WHOLE DAY OR BE SWEATY FOR A WEEK?

DAY 72
day seventy-two

FUN FACT: Most humans have 32 permanent teeth!

WOULD YOU RATHER... EAT ONLY GREEN FOODS OR EAT ONLY WHITE FOODS?

Why don't sharks eat clowns?

They taste funny!

DAY 73
day seventy-three

What do you give a lemon when its sick?

A lemon-aide!

WOULD YOU RATHER... HAVE A MAGIC WAND THAT TURNS THINGS INTO CANDY OR BRINGS YOUR TOYS TO LIFE?

FUN FACT: Butterflies can't fly if they are too cold!

DAY 74
day seventy-four

How do you clean a pig's feet?

Use ham sanitizer!

FUN FACT: One bee will only make a half teaspoon of honey!

WOULD YOU RATHER... HAVE A CAT THAT TELLS ALL YOUR SECRETS OR A DOG THAT WON'T STOP SINGING?

DAY 75
day seventy-five

FUN FACT:
Fairy Flies are the smallest insect!

WOULD YOU RATHER... WEAR A CHICKEN SUIT OR A CLOWN COSTUME TO SCHOOL?

Why did the deer go to the dentist?

It had buck teeth!

DAY 76
day seventy-six

What did the mommy cow say to the baby cow?

It's pasture bedtime!

WOULD YOU RATHER... HAVE BUBBLE GUM THAT NEVER LOSES ITS FLAVOR OR A COTTON CANDY TREE?

FUN FACT: About 350 pizza slices are eaten every second in the US.

GUM

DAY 77
day seventy-seven

How many tickles does it take to make an octopus laugh?

Ten-tickles!

FUN FACT: The first iPhone was released in 2007.

WOULD YOU RATHER... SNEEZE GLITTER OR HICCUP BUBBLES?

DAY 78
day seventy-eight

FUN FACT:
Sharks can't get cavities like humans!

WOULD YOU RATHER...
HAVE A UNICORN THAT POOPS RAINBOWS OR A DRAGON THAT BURPS TINY BALLS OF FIRE?

Why do bananas wear sunscreen?

Because they peel!

DAY 79
day seventy-nine

Why did the dinosaur cross the road?

The chicken wasn't born yet!

WOULD YOU RATHER... SLEEP IN A BED OF MARSHMALLOWS OR ON A PILLOW OF FLUFFY PANCAKES?

FUN FACT: Ice pops were invented by an 11 year old!

DAY 80
day eighty

What do you call two birds who are in love?

Tweethearts!

FUN FACT: Tigers have striped skin and striped fur!

WOULD YOU RATHER... HAVE A SMILE THAT LIGHTS UP LIKE A DISCO BALL OR EYEBROWS THAT WIGGLE?

DAY 81
day eighty-one

WOULD YOU RATHER... HAVE A TALKING SANDWICH THAT TELLS JOKES OR A SINGING SODA THAT SINGS SILLY SONGS?

FUN FACT: An ostrich's eye is bigger than its brain!

What type of music do planets listen to?

Neptunes!

DAY 82
day eighty-two

Why did the phone wear glasses?

It lost its contacts!

WOULD YOU RATHER... HAVE A NEVER-ENDING SUPPLY OF ICE CREAM OR A PLANT THAT GROWS A DOLLAR A DAY?

FUN FACT: The first version of Minecraft was release in 2011!

DAY 83
day eighty-three

Why do dragons sleep during the day?

They like to fight knights!

FUN FACT: Bees have 5 eyes and 6 legs!

WOULD YOU RATHER... EAT ALL YOUR FOOD BLENDED IN A MILKSHAKE OR NEVER EAT SWEETS AGAIN?

DAY 84
day eighty-four

FUN FACT:
Sloths are actually strong swimmers!

WOULD YOU RATHER... SWIM WITH AN OCTOPUS OR PLAY IN THE SAND WITH A CRAB?

What do you give a scientist with bad breath?

Experi-mints.

DAY 85
day eighty-five

What's worse than finding a worm in your apple?

Half a worm!

PEANUT BUTTER

WOULD YOU RATHER... WASH YOUR HAIR WITH KETCHUP OR WASH YOUR FACE WITH PEANUT BUTTER?

FUN FACT: A cat's ear has 32 muscles!

DAY 86
day eighty-six

Why did the nose feel sad?

It was getting picked on!

FUN FACT: ketchup used to be sold as a medicine!

WOULD YOU RATHER... EVERYTHING SMELL LIKE PIZZA OR EVERYTHING TASTES LIKE LEMONADE?

DAY 87
day eighty-seven

FUN FACT: The killer whale is in the dolphin family!

WOULD YOU RATHER... WEAR SHOES THAT ARE TOO BIG OR SOCKS THAT ARE TOO SMALL?

What do you call a shoe made out of a banana?

A slipper.

DAY 88
day eighty-eight

Where do books hide when they are scared?

Under the covers!

WOULD YOU RATHER... SLEEP UPSIDE DOWN LIKE A BAT OR IN A NEST LIKE A BIRD?

FUN FACT: A dime has 118 ridges around the edge!

DAY 89
day eighty-nine

What is a tornado's favorite game?

Twister.

FUN FACT: The first flight by airplane was in 1903!

WOULD YOU RATHER... EXPLORE A DARK CAVE WITH SPIDERWEBS OR EXPLORE A DEEP LAKE WITH SNAKES?

DAY 90
day ninety

WOULD YOU RATHER... SNORT EVERY TIME YOU LAUGH OR SQUEAK EVERY TIME YOU BLINK?

FUN FACT: Baby turtles are on their own after they hatch!

Why don't vampires have friends?

They are a pain in the neck!

DAY 91
day ninety-one

What do birds says on Halloween?

Trick or Tweet.

WOULD YOU RATHER...
SPIN IN CIRCLES WHEN YOU RUN OR JUMP WHEN YOU WALK?

FUN FACT:
A blob of toothpaste is called a nurdle!

DAY 92
day ninety-two

What is a
cat's favorite
color?

Purrr-ple.

FUN FACT:
Dogs have
dreams too!

WOULD YOU
RATHER...
DANCE WHEN
SOMEONE SAYS
HELLO OR
SING "HAPPY
BIRTHDAY" WHEN
A PHONE RINGS?

DAY 93
day ninety-three

FUN FACT:
The shortest war lasted 38 minutes!

WOULD YOU RATHER... HAVE A ROOM FULL OF RUBBER DUCKS OR A ROOM FULL OF SOCKS?

What has four wheels and flies?

A garbage truck.

DAY 94
day ninety-four

What falls in winter but never gets hurt?

-mous

WOULD YOU RATHER...
HAVE A TALKING BACKPACK THAT GIVES YOU ADVICE OR A LUNCHBOX THAT TELLS JOKES?

FUN FACT:
A guinea pig went to space in 1961!

DAY 95
day ninety-five

What do cakes and baseball have in common?

They both need a good batter!

FUN FACT:
Sea turtles can live for 50 – 100 years or more!

WOULD YOU RATHER... LAUGH FOR 5 HOURS OR DANCE THE WHOLE TIME AT A GROCERY STORE?

DAY 96
day ninety-six

FUN FACT:
Scientists use drones to catch whale snot for research!

WOULD YOU RATHER... HAVE A SILLY NAME OR HAVE CRAZY HAIR?

What do you call an elephant and a fish?

Swimming Trunks.

DAY 97
day ninety-seven

Why didn't the teddy bear want dessert?

It was stuffed.

WOULD YOU RATHER... BE SOMEONE'S PET LIZARD OR SOMEONE'S PET GOLDFISH?

FUN FACT: Australia is wider than the moon!

DAY 98
day ninety-eight

How much did the pirate pay for his flag?

It was on sale!

FUN FACT: A bumblebee bat is the smallest mammal!

WOULD YOU RATHER... BE A CHICKEN FOR A DAY OR A GOAT FOR A DAY?

DAY 99
day ninety-nine

FUN FACT:
The longest
English word
is 189,819
letters long!

WOULD YOU
RATHER...
WEAR A GLOW-
IN-THE-DARK
TUXEDO OR
WEAR A TUTU
THAT DROPS
GLITTER?

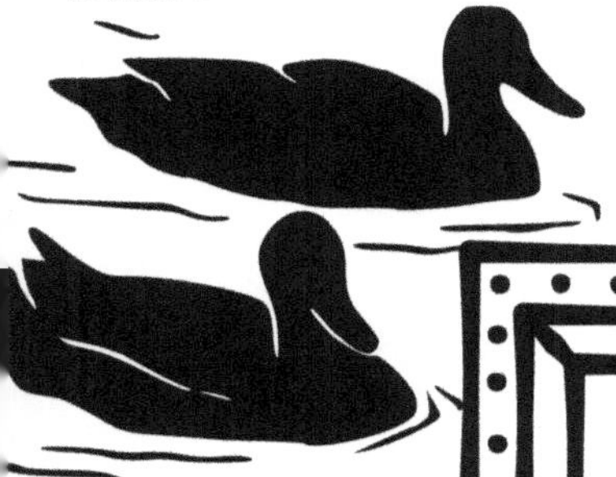

What do you
call 2 ducks
and a cow?

Quackers and milk!

DAY 100
day one hundred

Where do crayons go on vacation?

Color-ado.

WOULD YOU RATHER... SING A SILLY SONG IN FRONT OF 100 PEOPLE OR DO A SILLY DANCE IN FRONT OF 50 PEOPLE?

FUN FACT: Astronauts can make tools in space using 3D printing!

DAY 101
day one hundred one

What is a monster's favorite dessert?

I scream.

FUN FACT: The White House has its own movie theater!

WOULD YOU RATHER... DRIVE A SLOW BUT COOL CAR OR RIDE A RUSTY BUT FAST BIKE?

My Favorite Jokes

HEY, YOU ARE FUNNY TOO! WRITE YOUR JOKES
HERE TO MAKE THE HAHA HANDBOOK COMPLETE!

www.ingramcontent.com/pod-product-compliance
Lightning Source LLC
Chambersburg PA
CBHW051542120626
46551CB00013B/1337